## Crafting with Nature

# GO WILD!

## Science and Craft Projects with Animals

By Ruth Owen

**Enslow**
PUBLISHING

Published in 2024 by Enslow Publishing, LLC
2544 Clinton Street
Buffalo, NY 14224

Copyright © 2024 by The Rosen Publishing Group, Inc.

Portions of this work were originally authored by Ruth Owen and published as *Science and Craft Projects with Wildlife*. All new material this edition authored by Ruth Owen.

Produced for Rosen by Ruby Tuesday Books Ltd
Editor for Ruby Tuesday Books Ltd: Mark J. Sachner
Designer: Emma Randall

Manufactured in the United States of America

CPSIA compliance information: Batch #CSENS24: For further information contact
Enslow Publishing LLC, New York, New York at 1-800-398-2504.

Please visit our website, www.enslowpublishing.com. For a free color catalog of all our high-quality books,
call toll free 1-800-398-2504 or fax 1-877-980-4454.
————
Cataloging-in-Publication Data

Names: Owen, Ruth.
Title: Go wild!: science and craft projects with animals / Ruth Owen.
Description: New York : Enslow Publishing, 2024. | Series: Crafting with nature | Includes glossary and index.
Identifiers: ISBN 9781978535695 (pbk.) | ISBN 9781978535701 (library bound) | ISBN 9781978535718 (ebook)
Subjects: LCSH: Animals--Juvenile literature. | Nature study--Juvenile literature. | Handicraft--Juvenile literature.
Classification: LCC QL49.O94 2024 | DDC 745.592--dc23

Photo Credits:
Cover, 1, 4–5, 6–7, 8, 10–11, 14–15, 18–19, 20, 22–23, 26–27, 31 © Shutterstock;
9, 12–13, 16–17, 21, 24–25, 27 (bottom), 28–29 © Ruby Tuesday Books.

Find us on

# CONTENTS

# WILDLIFE ALL AROUND

If you live in the countryside you might see wild animals every day. But if you live in a city or town, you might think there is not much **wildlife** in your neighborhood. But wild animals are never that far away!

Birds, frogs, chipmunks, squirrels, raccoons, or foxes may be living in your backyard or in a nearby park. If you live in the country, you might have deer or coyotes as wildlife neighbors.

This book is all about the wild animals that live in our towns, cities, and countrysides. You will find out how they survive and raise their young. You will also get the chance to make some cool wildlife crafts!

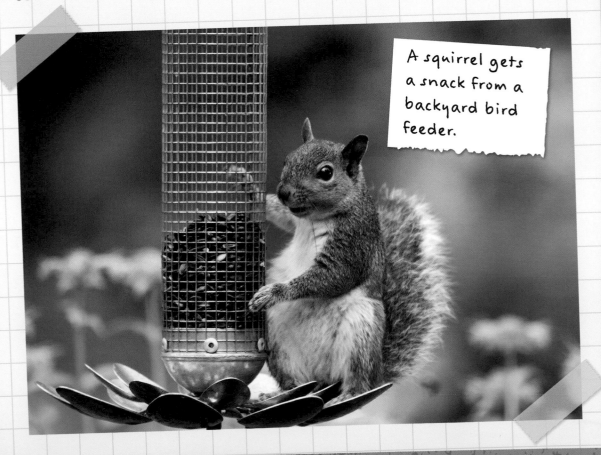

A squirrel gets a snack from a backyard bird feeder.

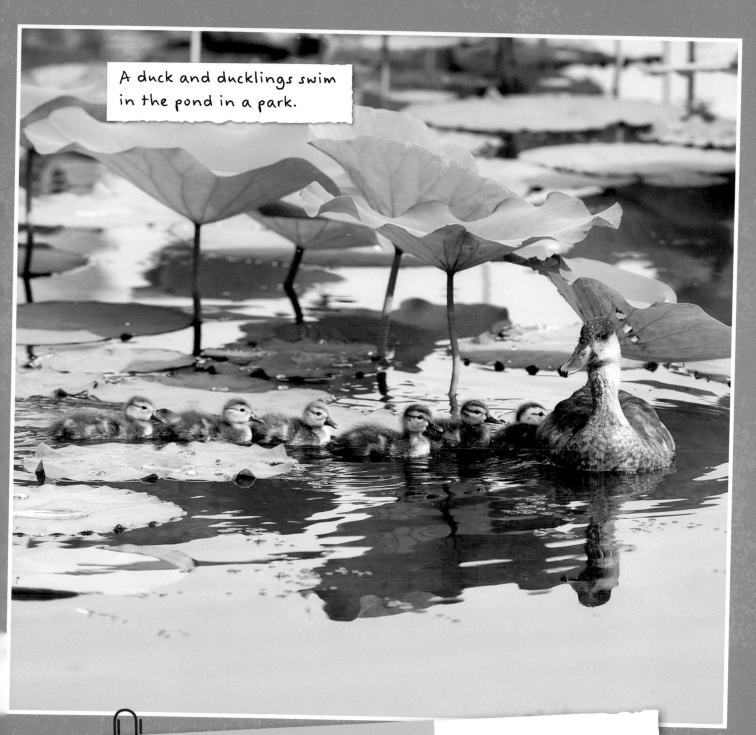

A duck and ducklings swim in the pond in a park.

## Animal Habitats

The area where an animal lives is called its **habitat**. A habitat might be as large as a forest or as small as a garden pond. In its habitat, an animal must be able to find water and food. It also needs a safe home where it can raise its young, find shelter from weather, and hide from enemies.

# IT'S TIME
# TO BUILD A NEST

When spring arrives, it's a busy time for wild birds. They pair up and start building nests for their eggs. You might get lucky and spot birds collecting nesting materials such as grass, twigs, and mud.

nest material

robin

After a male and female robin **mate**, the female builds a nest in a tree or thick bush. She makes the nest from twigs and grass. She might also use feathers and pieces of paper trash.

The nest is a safe place for the robin to lay her eggs. Then she sits on the eggs to keep them warm.

robin egg

nest

robin chicks

nest

After about 14 days, the robin chicks hatch from the eggs. They live in the nest until they are two weeks old and are strong enough to fly.

swallow chick

## Mud Nests

Different kinds of birds build different types of nests. Swallows collect mud in their beaks from the edges of ponds and streams. Then they use the mud to build their nests.

mud nest

# CRAFT A BIRD'S NEST

**How hard do birds have to work to build a nest? Find out with this first fun craft project.**

**You will need:**
- A bag for collecting nesting material
- Twigs
- Dry grass
- Moss
- Leaves
- Pieces of paper or cardboard trash
- Feathers
- Garden soil and water to make mud
- Sheets of newspaper

## GET CRAFTING:

**1** Collect materials to build a nest from your backyard, schoolyard, or a park.

dry grass

twigs

feathers

moss

dry leaves

**2** Remember, you can only use materials that you find in the wild. Birds can't visit a craft store to buy string or tape!

paper or cardboard trash

3 Place sheets of newspaper on a table or countertop and lay out all the materials you have found.

4 Use the twigs to make a framework for the nest. Try weaving them together to make a bowl shape.

5 Use grass, moss, and feathers to pad out the inside of the nest. If you wish, you can mix soil and water to make mud. Smear the mud onto the nest and use it like glue to hold the other nest materials together.

6 When you have finished making your nest, ask an adult to help you place it in a tree or bush—just like a real bird's nest!

7 Always wash your hands with hot water and soap after working with materials you find outdoors.

## Busy Birds

Did you find it difficult or easy to build a nest? Remember, you were able to use your hands. A bird must build its nest using its beak and feet. Also, a bird cannot collect all its nest materials at once. It has to make hundreds of journeys to collect the materials it needs.

# MEET THE RACCOONS

**Spring is also the time of year when squirrels, raccoons, and other mammals have babies.**

Female raccoons give birth to their cubs, or kits, in a safe home called a den. Raccoons build dens in holes in trees. Sometimes they make dens in spaces under the roofs of houses.

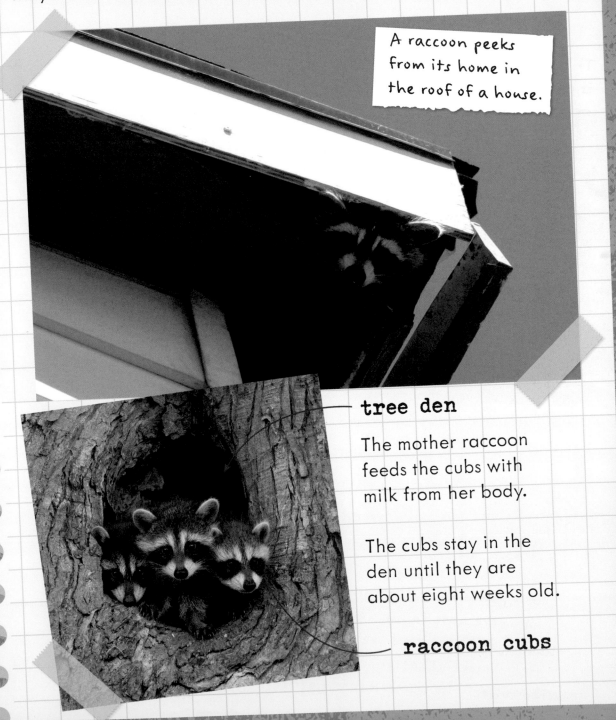

A raccoon peeks from its home in the roof of a house.

**tree den**

The mother raccoon feeds the cubs with milk from her body.

The cubs stay in the den until they are about eight weeks old.

**raccoon cubs**

When the cubs leave the den, they learn how to climb trees.

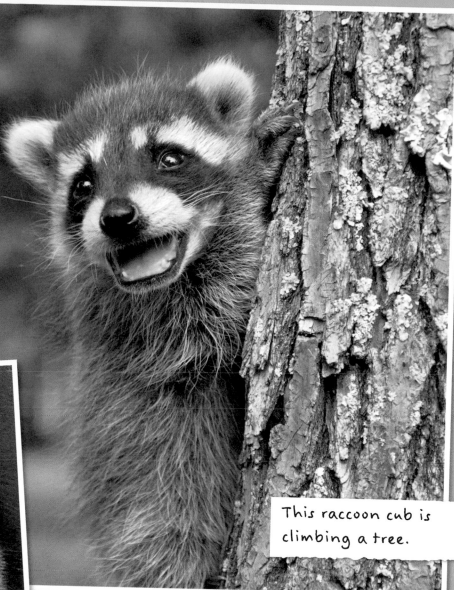

This raccoon cub is eating a plant.

This raccoon cub is climbing a tree.

The mother raccoon teaches the cubs how to find food such as fruit, plants, eggs, and **insects.**

## Smart Food Thieves

Raccoons sometimes steal dog or cat food from the porches of houses. They also look in garbage cans to find leftover human food.

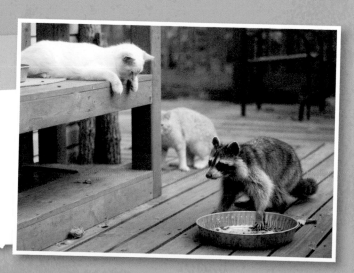

# A RACCOON DISGUISE

The black patches of fur on a raccoon's face make the little animal look like it's wearing a mask. This project shows you how to make your own raccoon disguise.

**You will need:**
- A paper plate
- Gray paint
- A paintbrush
- Scissors
- A piece of cardboard
- Glue
- Black felt
- Pink felt
- A wooden stick or tongue depressor
- 6 white drinking straws
- Tape
- Chalk
- An adult to help with cutting

## GET CRAFTING:

1   Paint the paper plate gray.

Ask an adult to help you cut two triangles from the cardboard to make ears. Paint the ears gray. When the paint is dry, glue the ears to the paper plate.

2   Cut two small triangles from the black felt and glue these to the ears. Make sure an adult helps you cut the felt shapes for your mask.

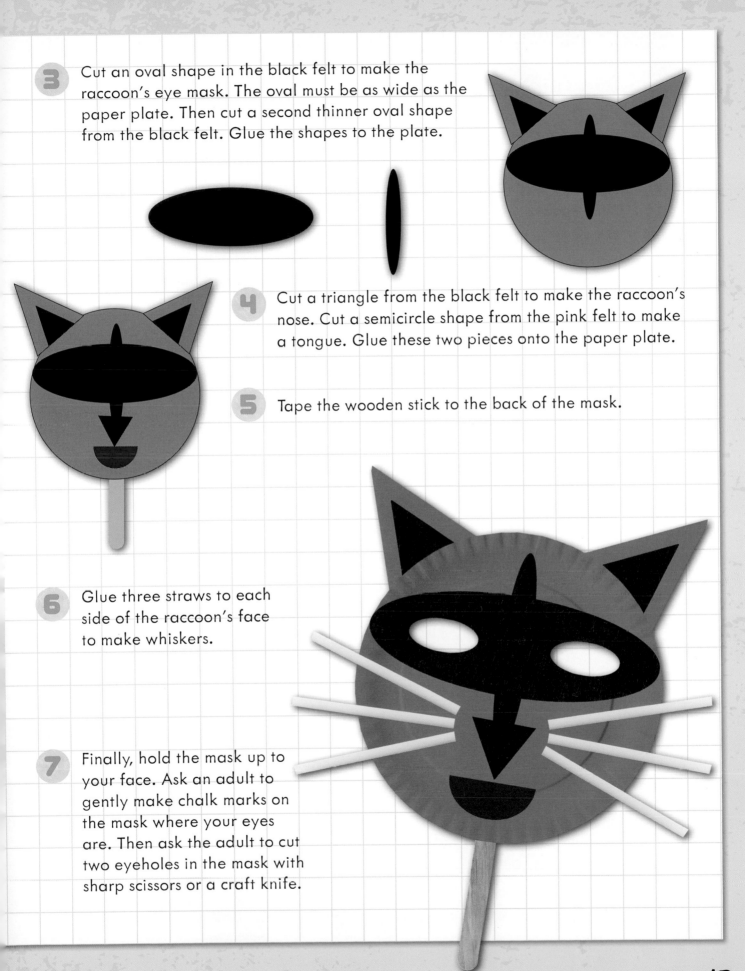

**3** Cut an oval shape in the black felt to make the raccoon's eye mask. The oval must be as wide as the paper plate. Then cut a second thinner oval shape from the black felt. Glue the shapes to the plate.

**4** Cut a triangle from the black felt to make the raccoon's nose. Cut a semicircle shape from the pink felt to make a tongue. Glue these two pieces onto the paper plate.

**5** Tape the wooden stick to the back of the mask.

**6** Glue three straws to each side of the raccoon's face to make whiskers.

**7** Finally, hold the mask up to your face. Ask an adult to gently make chalk marks on the mask where your eyes are. Then ask the adult to cut two eyeholes in the mask with sharp scissors or a craft knife.

13

**If you're lucky enough to live near a pond, carefully take a look in spring and you might spot frogs laying their eggs.**

After mating, a female frog lays thousands of eggs in water. Each tiny black egg is inside a blob of see-through jelly.

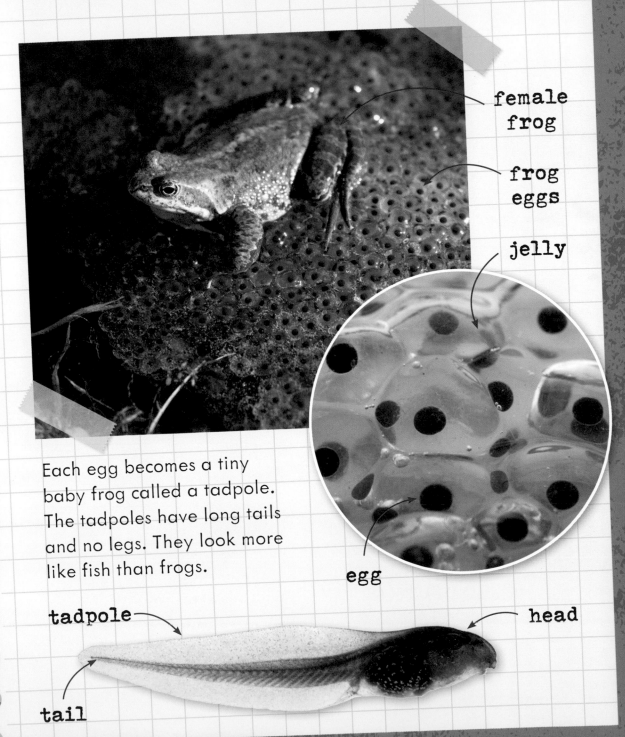

female frog

frog eggs

jelly

egg

Each egg becomes a tiny baby frog called a tadpole. The tadpoles have long tails and no legs. They look more like fish than frogs.

tadpole

head

tail

14

The tadpoles go through lots of changes. First they grow back legs. Then they grow front legs. Their tails get shorter, too.

back leg

back leg    front leg

short tail

adult frog

Finally, the tadpoles' tails disappear and they become adult frogs!

## How Do Tadpoles Breathe?

A frog uses its **lungs** to breathe **oxygen** from the air, like you. A tadpole can only breathe underwater, like a fish. It uses body parts called **gills** to take oxygen out of the water. As it changes into a frog, a tadpole grows lungs for breathing air.

# MAKE A FROGGY COLLAGE

In this next project you can make a collage of the life cycle of a frog. A life cycle shows the stages of an animal's life. A frog's life cycle starts with an egg. Next, it becomes a tadpole. Then the tadpole grows into an adult frog that can mate and make more eggs so the cycle begins again.

## You will need:
- A large piece of cardboard
- Scissors
- Aluminum foil
- Green construction paper, felt, or scraps of fabric
- White construction paper
- 3 black buttons
- A piece of red or pink ribbon or string
- Colorful buttons to make spots
- Glue
- Bubble wrap
- Black marker
- Brown paper
- Red paper
- An adult to be your teammate and to help with cutting

## GET CRAFTING:

**1** Ask an adult to help you cut the large piece of cardboard into a circle to make a pond background. Cover the cardboard circle with aluminum foil.

**2** To make the frog's head and body, cut two circles from green construction paper, felt, or fabric. Ask an adult to help you with the cutting.

16

**3** Draw the frog's feet onto the green paper or fabric and cut them out.

**4** Cut two small circles from the white construction paper.

**5** Now glue all the frog pieces onto the pond. Add two black buttons to the frog's eyes and a ribbon mouth. You can glue on extra buttons to give your frog spotty skin.

**6** Glue some bubble wrap to the pond. Use the marker to add black dots for eggs.

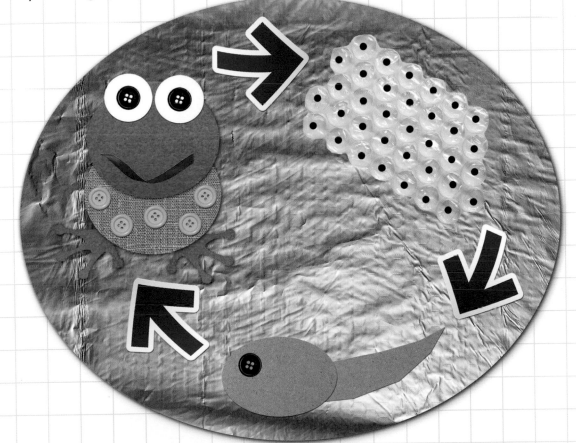

**7** To make the tadpole, cut an oval from the brown paper. Cut a long shape to make the tadpole's tail. Glue the tadpole pieces onto the pond. Add a black button eye.

**8** Add paper arrows to the frog life cycle.

# WHAT DO BIRDS EAT?

**From dawn to dusk, wild birds are busy searching for food.**

Some birds, such as waxwings, mainly eat **seeds**, berries, and fruit.

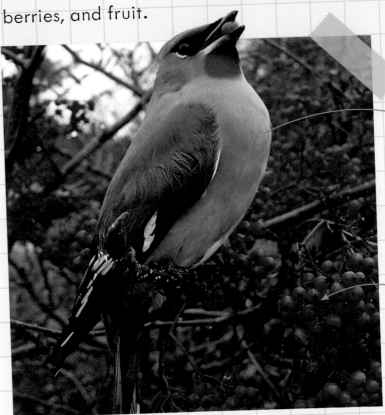

waxwing

berries

Other birds, such as robins, eat grasshoppers, caterpillars, and other insects. They also eat small animals such as worms.

robin

worm

In winter it can be difficult for wild birds to find enough food. Most plants do not produce seeds or fruit in winter. Also, there are few insects around.

bird feeder

cardinal

People can help wild birds in winter by giving them food. Nuts, sunflower seeds, and food scraps can be placed on a bird table. Bird feeders filled with seeds can be hung in trees.

## Be a Bird-Watcher

Watch the birds in your garden, backyard, or nearby park.
Try to spot the following:
• A bird eating seeds or berries from a plant.
• A bird with a worm in its beak.
• A bird looking under leaves to find insects.
• A bird drinking water from a pond, puddle, or birdbath.

# PINE CONE FEEDER

It's possible to turn a pine cone into an energy-packed feeder for the hungry wild birds in your neighborhood.

**You will need:**

- Large pine cone with open scales
- Vegetable shortening
- Wild birdseed (from a pet store)
- Other ingredients, which may include crushed fresh peanuts (not roasted or salted), stale bread, cake, cookie crumbs, cheese crumbs, or dried fruit
- A measuring cup

- A spoon
- A plate
- 4 feet (1.2 m) of string
- An adult teammate to help you go pinecone gathering and help you tie your bird feeder to a tree branch

## GET CRAFTING:

1. You can visit a park or forest where there are pine trees to find pine cones. It's also possible to buy pine cones from craft stores.

2. Tie one end of the string around the top of the pine cone.

pine cone

open scales

Pour one cup of wild birdseed and the other ingredients onto the plate.

**wild birdseed**

**dried fruit**

**cookie crumbs**

4. Spread lots of shortening over the pine cone with the spoon.

5. Roll the shortening-covered pine cone in the seeds and other ingredients. Use the spoon to push lots of seed and shortening between the pine cone's scales. Try to pack as many goodies onto the pine cone as possible!

6. Ask an adult to help you tie the pine cone outside. A tree branch or a porch is a good place. Make sure you choose a place where cats cannot pounce on the birds as they feed.

7. Keep watch for birds visiting your feeder!

# WINTER FOOD STORES

Trees and other plants don't produce fruits or seeds in winter. So animals that eat these foods have to prepare by storing food for this tough time of year.

In the fall, squirrels collect acorns that drop from oak trees.

squirrel

They bury the acorns in the ground. Then, when there is no food around in winter, they dig up their buried food.

acorns

Chipmunks live in underground homes called burrows.

During the fall, a chipmunk collects thousands of nuts and seeds. It stores this food in its burrow.

Then the chipmunk spends the cold winter months sleeping in its burrow. If it gets hungry, it eats some of its stored food.

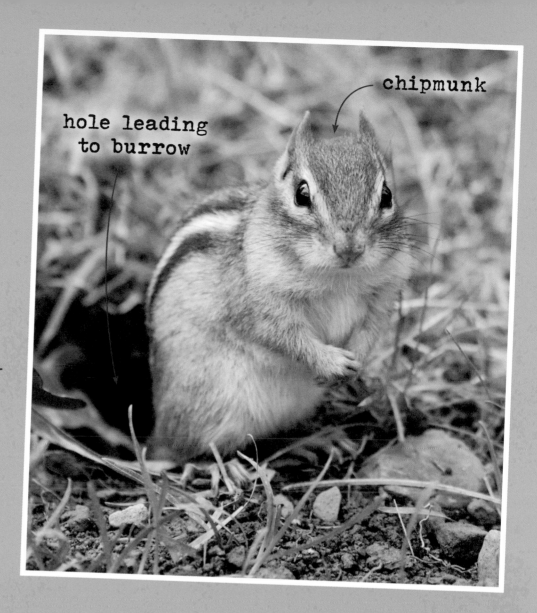

chipmunk

hole leading to burrow

cheek filled with food

## Chubby Chipmunk Cheeks

Chipmunks carry nuts and seeds in a **pouch** in each of their cheeks. A chipmunk can stuff about 60 sunflower seeds into each cheek pouch!

# CHIPMUNK TREAT JARS

Jars are always very useful for storing nuts, sunflower seeds, and other snack foods. So be a chipmunk and get storing your favorite treats in recycled jars with a toothy chipmunk theme.

**You will need:**
- Clean, empty jars with lids
- Glue
- Scissors
- Orange or dark brown felt
- Pale brown or yellow felt
- White felt
- Black felt
- Pink felt
- An adult to be your teammate and to help with cutting

## GET CRAFTING:

**1** You can use pickle, mayonnaise, or jam jars to make your storage jars.

**2** Take the lid off a jar and cover the outside of the lid with glue. Put glue around the sides of the lid, too.

**3** Lay the lid glue side down on a piece of orange felt that is slightly larger than the lid. Press down firmly. Then fold up the felt so that it sticks to the sides of the lid.

**4** Ask an adult to trim off any spare felt so the whole lid is neatly covered with felt. You now have your chipmunk's face.

**5** Cut these shapes from the orange, pale brown, black, white, and pink felt. Remember, the shapes must fit onto the lid, or face.

**6** Now glue the shapes onto the face. First, stick on the ears, eye patches, eyes, and teeth.

**7** Then glue on the two cheeks. Finally, glue on the nose.

**8** Allow the glue to dry. Your storage jar is ready to fill with goodies!

# SPOTTING WILDLIFE TRACKS

**One way to find out what animals live in your neighborhood is to look for tracks, or footprints.**

Animal tracks can show you what places an animal visited. You might even be able to follow the tracks to find out where the animal went next!

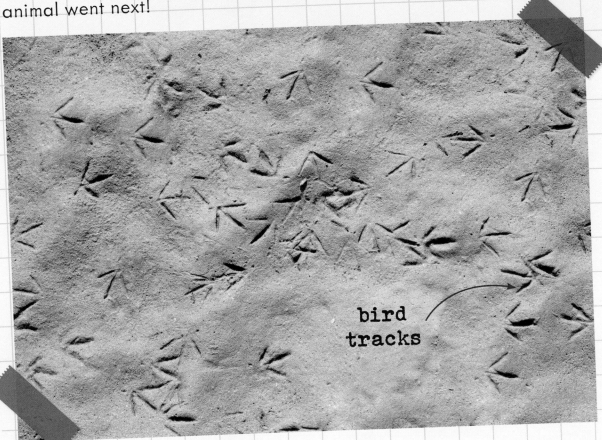

bird tracks

Look for tracks in mud or snow.

You might see muddy footprints on the hood of a car.

Animals may leave tracks in sand at a playground.

You can take photographs of the tracks you spot. Before you take the photograph, put a dime next to the track. This will show the real-life size of the footprint.

# GET TRACKING

squirrel · raccoon · bear

dog · cat · duck

## Making Tracks

On a dry day, try sprinkling a layer of flour on a flat surface in your garden or schoolyard. Then place a plate of food in the center. See page 20 for ideas of which foods to use. The next day, check the flour for tracks to see if birds or other animals have visited the food.

# ANIMAL TRACK CASTS

Keep a record of any large animal tracks you find by making a cast, or model, of them. The footprint will need to be in dried mud or sand. If you can't find a track, make your own in some modeling clay.

**You will need:**
- Plaster of Paris
- Water
- A bowl
- A spoon for mixing
- A paper clip

- A strip of cardboard about 18 inches (46 cm) long and 1 inch (2.5 cm) wide
- Modeling clay if you are making your own tracks

## GET CRAFTING:

**1** Find a track or make one in modeling clay.

**2** Using the cardboard strip and paper clip, make a little collar, or wall, around the track.

**3** You will need to make enough plaster mix to fill the collar. Put some plaster of Paris into the bowl and start adding water.

**4** Stir the mixture to remove any lumps. The mixture should be the thickness of pancake batter. Keep adding plaster or water until the mix is right.

**5** Start gently pouring the mix into the collar to the side of the print. Let the mix slowly run into the print so it doesn't damage its shape. Then fill the rest of the area inside the collar with mix.

**6** The plaster should set hard in about 30 minutes. Gently touch the plaster to find out if it is dry and hard. If it still feels soft, leave it for another 10 minutes and then try again.

**7** When the plaster is hard and dry, remove the collar. Very carefully lift up the model using two hands on opposite sides of the model. On the underside of the model will be a cast of the footprint!

**8** Allow the cast to dry out for three or four more days before cleaning or painting it.

**9** If you need to clean dirt or sand from the model, hold it under a slow-flowing tap. Let the water gently wash off the dirt. When the model has dried out again, you can paint it if you wish.

# GLOSSARY

**gills** (GILZ)
Body parts that some water animals, such as fish and tadpoles, use for breathing.

**habitat** (HA-buh-tat)
The place where an animal or plant normally lives. A habitat may be a backyard, a forest, the ocean, or a pond in a park.

**insect** (IN-sekt)
A small animal with six legs, a body in three parts, and a hard outer shell, called an exoskeleton.

**lungs** (LUNGZ)
Body parts that humans and other animals use for breathing air.

**mammal** (MA-mul)
A warm-blooded animal that has a backbone and usually has hair. Mammals give birth to live babies and feed them milk from their bodies.

**mate** (MAYT)
When a male and female come together to produce young.

**oxygen** (OK-sih-jen)
A gas in the air that is needed by humans and other animals for breathing.

**pouch** (POWCH)
A body part that's a little like a pocket.

**seed** (SEED)
A part of a plant that contains all the material needed to grow a new plant.

**wildlife** (WYLD-lyf)
Animals that live wild in their natural habitat and are not pets, farm animals, or zoo animals.

## Websites

https://kids.nationalgeographic.com/animals

https://www.nwf.org/Kids-and-Family/Connecting-Kids-and-Nature

https://www.audubon.org/get-outside/activities/audubon-for-kids

# READ MORE

**Klatte, Kathleen A.** *Raccoons at Night (Up All Night! Nocturnal Animals)*. New York, NY: Rosen Publishing, 2021.

**Mattern, Joanne.** *Fantastic Homes for Flying Creatures (Wildlife Rescue)*. Minneapolis, MN: Red Chair Press, 2023.

**Owen, Ruth.** *Welcome to the City at Night (Nature's Neighborhoods: All About Ecosystems)*. Minneapolis, MN: Ruby Tuesday Books, 2023.

# INDEX